tell
me
another
story

tell
me
another
story

poems of you and me

emmy marucci

Andrews McMeel
PUBLISHING®

"we are, as a species, addicted to story. even when the body goes to sleep, the mind stays up all night, telling itself stories."

—jonathan gottschall

for my buddy

preface

the time was around christmas. i was young, probably 5. i fell asleep
on the carpet of my grandmother's house, a new toy beside me and
a furnace-warmed blanket over me. on the walls were paintings of a
snowy scene, old-fashioned cars and an old man, wrinkles and circles
under his eyes. on the floor was a trumpet beside a reclining chair.

i remember opening and closing my eyes and catching glimpses of
people standing around my grandfather. he was wearing a brightly
colored polo sweater, a cap, a ring on his pinky finger. his hands
danced—up and down and clasped and high in the air and on the table
and over people's shoulders and grasping at their hands. all eyes were
intently focused on him. no interruptions. just the faint sound of music
in the background and the smell of linguine with clams wafting in from
the kitchen. the most striking thing, really, all these years later, remains
the insanely beautiful feeling in the room. big. enormous. in my gut.
stuck in my heart. i don't know if he was telling a joke or a story. it was
always one or the other. but what he was doing was an act to be taken
seriously. a performance. like singing a song. you should listen and learn
and feel. you should live in the moment for as long as possible.

my mom has always said that i was born a storyteller. i suppose i was.
our family revolves around the giving, the telling, and the sharing. the
extending of our voices, the championing of our words. my grandfather,
buddy, or pop, passed away while i was writing this book. to me, he
was everybody and everything i have ever known. and because of that,
much of this book is about the pain of losing him—an experiment
in truly and honestly listening to myself. but it also consists of my
interpretations of other people's stories—an experiment in listening to
those who surround me.

the title of this book reminds me of what a child might ask of his mother at bedtime, to avoid having to go to sleep. it reminds me of how you feel when someone you love is dying—the wanting to know more. the wanting them to stay and tell you everything, again and again. the wanting to remember all the stories you fear you might forget.

if one thing is true, it's that storytelling is universal. we hear our first story when we're in the womb, a quiet witness to it all. as we grow, we yearn for more—more once-upon-a-times, fairy tales, and folk stories. storytelling exists throughout our lives. steady. like a heartbeat. we become hunters and gatherers, passing down information. some stories stay with us and never leave. eternal. i can still see my grandfather from the corner of my eye, the back of him, moving, his voice expanding and shifting, his words. this book is made of a few of my own stories. and a few of yours. transcendent and worth telling.

**don't
leave
just yet**
tell me
another
story

part one
me

go on and grieve

you roll into the hospital room
i notice
you look more wrinkled than
last weekend

i get close
in case you can't see me

put my hand through your hair
and run my fingers over
your eyebrows

like mom did to me
when i was a baby

you're not gone yet
but this is what grieving
looks like

dustin holds your hand
and i
hold the other

we look at each other
and cry

it's like a song
we're singing

we stay by your bedside
keeping watch
while your eyes open and close
softly

you're mumbling things
and we're telling you
not to worry

that
everything is taken care of

i hold on to the
little of you that's in there

your toes tapping
under the hospital sheets

the way you tuck your thumb
into the middle of your other four fingers

when you whisper
to me
and tell me i am the most beautiful girl
you've ever seen

it's not the morphine
no
you're in there somewhere
i feel it

go on and grieve

drink the wine
and watch your tears
fall onto your french fries
at the restaurant on 7th avenue

stare off into the distance
for a while
until things get blurry
and look the way
your insides feel

leave the meetings
where you're talking about
button-up shirts
and linen pants
and be pissed
because you know
none of it matters

go ahead and fantasize about
delaying all your plans
even the wedding that's coming
in 3 months

because
next year things will be better

go to cvs
buy the bubble gum
that makes you feel like a kid
and let the rude cashier
make you sob on the way out

lie in your bathtub
don't wash your face
don't do anything, actually
just lie there
and watch how your hands float
every time you breathe in

stop in parking lots
and hold on to each other
while you weep

put on the song
that makes you feel
all the saddest things

"over the rainbow"
 or
"danny boy"
 or
the song he always played you

go ahead
and hum it
while you're walking through
the union square subway station

and feel that feeling
the tears coming up your throat
and swallow
swallow them
and hide
hide
if you want to hide

or
for fuck's sake
cry if you need to
all the time
in front of everyone

look like shit
with
hollowed-out eyes

and wear the same
white t-shirt
every day this week

stop eating if you so please
or eat all the mozzarella
and everything bagels
and potato chips
you can in one afternoon

and when you feel like
all has gone quiet

close your eyes and
sleep
sleep for a while

and dream
dream
dream

dream of better times

the music is gone

we left it on
glen road
i suppose

in the house with the red brick
the dried-up cicadas

in the front
that nana

tiptoed over
in the spring

in the house mom almost
burnt down
the day she made an ashtray
out of paper

the same house
where i'd fall asleep
on the carpet
in front of the tv

on christmas eve nights
while you all sang
carols

and spun around corners
dancing

holding
hands
fingertip to fingertip

the way two people
slow dance

come to think of it
it almost looked like
you all were praying

and if there was any religion
inside those walls at all

it was the music
coming from your horn

and if there ever was
a godly song

that heals people
from the inside

it had to be
when you played
"danny boy"

the only time everyone
stopped and stood
in one place

there was always something cooking
linguine of some kind

there were always
italian men with pinky rings

and whiskey
holding their bellies
laughing

and i would fall asleep on the carpet
and dream
of it always being that way

i never told you but
i was awake
when you put the warm blanket
from the radiator
over me

i never told you
i heard the joke about the whore
and i opened my eyes just enough

to watch everyone
as they drifted back and forth
between each other

happy

and well
now the people in that house
who i memorized
and dreamt about
have wrinkled hands

and the valves on the horn
are rusty

stuck

and no matter what i do
you'll die soon

or as you like to say
you'll take the train

but if it's you on that train
i want you to get off

at the next stop

i'll play all your favorite songs
loud

and i swear i'll sit for hours
watching your feet tap
ever so slightly
and i'll turn the volume up
louder
louder
louder

i'll learn how to cook
all your favorite dishes

i'll even brush your white hair
every day
the way i did
when i was young

but the truth is

we left the music on glen road
and whatever is left of it

i know

you'll take it with you
when you go

we cleaned out your closet

i keep the clothes
from your closet
in a big gift bag

i take the corners
and i fold the top over
so no air can get in

and once in a while
when no one's looking
i carefully unfold it
take the shirt that's on top out
put it up to my chest

i hug it
and i breathe in deeply

and there's that sweet smell
a mix of dove soap
and shaving cream

it's the only hint of you
i have left

it feels like you're here
in the room

again

and i feel happy

i put it back
neatly
and create that perfect
fold again

i need to make sure it's safe
the you that's still here

and then i cry
and cry
and cry

i wipe the tears
i wipe it all away

i put myself through this
ritual of pain

again
and
again
and
again
and
again

where are you?

we are watching videos of you
laughing
your hand on your belly

and i text mom

WHERE IS HE??!!

and mom texts back

i was just thinking that
watching the video of us dancing
and thinking

WHERE IS THIS BEING??

this force of nature
cannot be gone

suddenly
the oar hanging on the wall
falls off

was that you, pop?

you sad writer, you

you're taking the zoloft
and only writing about
your grandfather dying

you're crying
way too much

you're most definitely
fucking up
this whole book thing

but
what

what about the sun

the way it feels
on your skin

what about that time
you laughed

what about the fireflies
chasing your barefoot nephew
in the yard

what about that note in
your favorite song

what about the kiss
he gave you before work

that soft breeze
that made your hair dance

what about your tears
tickling your face

what about cheese
on top of pasta

and mom
and dad
and brothers

what about getting drunk on
rosé
and red wine
and tequila
and a little weed

and holding hands with
friends

what about that blue dress
that hangs in your closet

and the shoes
that match it perfectly

what about the bay
and the way it glows
when the sun sets

what about when kittens
curl up in tiny balls

what about
jamming out
to fleetwood mac
alone in your living room

and don't forget
about
rainbow sprinkles
and guacamole
not together
but separately

the smell of
jasmine
cedar
lavender
firepits

mom making pancakes
with blueberries
in the morning

and what about the words
how good they feel
when you put them on paper

write about that

it's like an ache

this loss
feels like
an ache
between my ribs

it's sad
and scary

but soft
and steady

it's always there
humming loudly
beneath it all

beneath it all

sometimes
it rests
and
just whispers

ssshhhhhhhh

it only takes
one
moment
of missing you
to make it roar

i must be getting old

i say to myself as i
walk down bleecker street

who knew
acid wash jeans were back in?

and wearing them
so low your pubes show?

not i

said the 30-year-old girl

(ahem!)
woman

whose high-rises
practically touch her nipples

whose eyes can't stay "woke"
past 10pm

what's "in" anyway?
i wonder

as i sip my cocktail
that's too strong
for this body
that's growing older
from one second to the next

what's "in"
i know

is getting super wrinkly
to the point that
you resemble a shar-pei

or like a peach that's
been sitting in the sun all summer long

what's "in" is
running out of books to read
and songs to sing

what's "in" is seeing your
great-grandkids

what's "in" is getting sick
then
getting better

and watching your hair
go from chestnut to white

what's "in" is keeping
that curiosity in your heart
and that hope in your pockets

for as long as you can
hold on

my gay uncle

"you walk like a girl"
they said to you
when you were a boy
on your way to school

that's the day
your eyes would change

we found you
40 years later
on new year's day
in your chair
a coffee cup in front of you
a cigarette still freshly burnt

i hope in heaven
they love you
for it

for that walk

different

beautiful

sick joke

mom dreams her brother comes
crashing through the front door

it was all a sick joke!
he never died!

he was just away for the weekend
shopping for silk pajamas at bloomingdale's
ordering white russians
charging it to pop's tab
going through packs of cigarettes
and putting pastels to canvas

she is angry
the kind of angry that's mixed with sad
scared
crazed
the *how could you do this to me?*
kind of angry

they say
departed family members visit you
for a number of reasons

unfinished business
unresolved grief
comfort
healing
the subconscious production of imagery
that relates to the familiar

the not being able to let go

poetry doesn't just come to me

i can sit at all the desks
in the world

light a nice-smelling candle
or the ends of a burnt palo santo bundle

i can listen to burroughs tell me
that he wrote from 10am to 6pm

every day
with no problem at all

but
then i remember

burroughs is a fucking god
if there ever was one

and i
just have to sit
and wait

for the people to come to me
the ones with the stories worth telling

with
the sad eyes looking at you
the wrinkled faces
the exchanging of words
the shaking of hands
the brief glances
the insane heartbreaks
the sharing of space

if it weren't for them
the people
there would be no poems
no books
no words

it'd just be me
and my barely beating heart
with nothing to say at all

how am i?

no one answers
the question
how are you?
truthfully

how am i?

i feel like the painting
the poetry of silence
by vilhelm hammershøi

oil on canvas
tears on the floor

busy bees

driving to work
sirens

a man with rubber gloves
looks defeated

beside him
blood

on the corner of canal
and 6th avenue

we're behind the ambulance
when i say
"there's someone fighting
for their life in there"

you say
"that's weird to think about"

you're right
and
we all go on

buzzing through the streets
beeping our horns
getting our coffees
checking off our lists
eating our apples
calling our taxis
and closing our apps

we've become so busy
we've forgotten to look around

explaining death to a 4-year-old

when our dog finn died
all the adults gathered
and talked about
how we might explain it to you

we read you a book called
dog heaven
it says that in heaven
there are
"fields to run in,
soft beds (made of clouds turned inside out)
where god has a sense of humor
and spends his time making puppy biscuits"

it was going well
until you asked
"well, can i see finn again?"
and of course
we replied no

your face grew worried
stern and serious
and you said

"i don't like heaven"

when our pop died
all the adults gathered
and talked about
how we might explain it to you

i remember you in your dad's arms
in front of the casket

he whispered in your ear
"now say goodbye to pop pop"
the sweetest little voice came out of you

"bye, pop pop"

but a little bit of time had gone by
in between
finn and pop passing
and you had forgotten
what it all meant

you asked
"well, can i see pop again?"
and of course
we replied no

your face grew worried
stern and serious
and you said

"i don't like heaven"

it is hard to believe that there
is anything more beautiful than
seeing you understand love
and sadness so wholly
and so completely

i've come to realize
maybe i don't like heaven either

my greatest fear is death

but here i am standing
right in front of you
watching it happen

you always told me
i'd have to get over it

it's part of life, you said
it happens to everyone, you said
you should not be afraid of the things
you cannot change, you said

but you didn't tell me about
the losing your mind part

the forgetting your spouse's name
who you've lived with for 60 years part

you didn't tell me about the
searching for your mom and dad
who have been gone for years and years part

about the shaking hands part
and the having to eat your salad with spoons part

about the cold hospital sheets part

and the humming of machines
and the shitty mushroom soup
that the nurses serve at weird times of day part

the morphine part

the shifting of your body
so it doesn't bruise part

the fluorescent lights
the agony
coming from the neighboring rooms part

you never told me
about the time it would take
painful
long
too long
part

about the eyes part
you didn't tell me that your eyes
would look different

here
but
not
here
at the same time

i'm beginning to think
this fear is valid

i think you'd agree

i'd tell you the
story of how it went
in the end

and
you'd look at me
with a beer in your hand
a frank sinatra song in the background
and some pasta on the table waiting to be eaten

and you'd say
fuck that
that death thing
and we'd drink
drink
drink
and sing
sing
sing
and laugh

laugh
laugh
as if there weren't a chance
it could ever happen
to us

as if we could live in the moment forever
hand in hand
music loud
hearts beating
bodies strong

right here
where all is right

you and me

here
here
forever

totally drunk
and
totally and completely
alive

youth

dating the basketball player
and making love in his upstairs bedroom
while his mother cooks
chicken cutlets below us

throwing parties in empty houses
with for-sale signs in the front yard
and being shoved into the closet
with your girlfriend
while the boy on the other side
screams "make out!"

smoking hookahs with weed
crumpled up inside tinfoil balls
making o's as we exhale
the smoke

groups of girls
staring each other
up and down
from either side of the driveway

walking home barefoot
early in the morning
soaking our feet
in hot bathwater

dressing up in black
dipping tampons into
cranberry juice
and spreading them about town

combing our necks
until the hickeys
disappear

taking dad's mercedes out to get
ping-pong balls down the street at cvs

not knowing how to change gears
in the parking lot
our hands pressing buttons
and jerking the wheel

stuck

sipping bacardi o
in weird musty basements
where virginities are lost

boyfriends' sweatshirts
and doodles in composition books
and folded-up notes
read a hundred times over

the intense range of emotion
the great feeling of sadness
the longing
the future feeling so vast
the not knowing who the fuck you are
the believing that we'll always look this way
feel this way
the late nights of recklessness
the making of mistakes
the naivety of it all

youth
it leaves you quick
and it never comes back

selfish me

for being so sad
about the death of my
93-year-old grandfather

when babies have to leave us
before they've had a
chance to be born

when fathers
grow tumors inside
their brains
at 49 years young

when the teenage boy can't
quit taking the pills
he's bought on the street

when the healthy runner's
heart stops beating
and she falls to the floor

when the lungs of a woman
who's never smoked
a cigarette in her life
turn black

when the football player
who was once
all muscle
is paralyzed
from the neck down

when the mom
who wants a better life
gets separated from her 2-year-old
at the border

when a man loves
another man
and his parents can't
look him in the eye

when the black boy
is shot for pretending
to be a cowboy
at the playground

when you can't go to
a country concert or
movie theater or
marathon or
nightclub or
your high school classroom
without fearing for your life

when there are daughters
who walk down aisles
alone

when there are crashes
and cancers
and fires that burn near beaches

when there are
aching bodies
snaky politicians

wrecked cars
starving mouths
cold hands, feet
and hearts
silenced voices
melting ice caps
fizzling stars

selfish me

when there are
so many sad stories
sadder than my own

grief moves like the moon

it goes through phases

sometimes it's a sliver
waning
the darkness creeping in from the right
when you least expect it

sometimes it takes up more space
waxing
you feel it just after the sun sets
when you have a minute to sit down and think

sometimes it's full
illuminating everything
because the sun and the moon
have moved close to each other in the sky

you
and
me

so
close
but
so
so
far

nurse kevin

my mother and grandmother
are talking with the social worker
down the hall

i'm with you alone
rubbing your frozen hands

i have rubber gloves on
that smell like alcohol
and i am trying not to cry

the worst thing would be to cry
right in front of you

the hospital walls are the ugliest color
dirty almond milk
and everything has a sick smell

bitter

mom has always said
that sick has a smell
and now i understand

the rhythm of the monitor
is enough to make anyone crazy

you start to get agitated
you want to get up
and escape this whole thing

it seems to me that you know
where you are going
and you want to run
in the opposite direction

but you are strong, pop
you are strong

i can feel it
you want to
take that thin backless robe off
throw it down to the ground
put on your yellow polo sweater
grab your wallet
that you always tie with a rubber band
put on your pinky ring with the stone
that moves like the ocean

and get the hell out of here
as quick as you can

you are strong, pop
you are strong

your will
and your body
are listening to each other
for the first time in months

it scares me
that i can't keep you in bed

i call for nurse kevin
and leave the room

i do this thing
where i am almost laughing
because i am so scared
and so uncomfortable

embarrassed
i fall to the floor and
put my face into my hands

i hear kevin saying softly

"buddy!"
his voice calm

"let's talk about the music.
you're a trumpet player, right?"

where did he come from?
how can someone be so beautiful?

changing soaked sheets
rubbing tense shoulders
wiping down bodies

squeezing blood from gauze
feeling foreheads for fevers
sending medicine through clear tubes

spooning pudding into mouths
wrapping bodies in warm blankets
keeping close watch over heartbeats

listening to last breaths
listening to last rites

we heard he visited pop on his day off
why?

i will give him the book
the language of kindness: a nurse's story
after pop passes

and i will think of him every time
i see a nurse on the train
tired
nodding off
the bottoms of their scrubs
worn and fraying

and i will think
where did they come from?
how can someone be so beautiful?

the uber driver

you and me
we are strangers

i'm drunk
and we're dancing

you from lebanon
and me from jersey

we're friends in the night
moving to the same song
swaying our hands in the same breeze
breathing the same air freshener

it's these moments
that make me feel human
again

tenderly

it's may and i'm cooking
turkey chili

charlie spivak's
"tenderly"
plays on the record player

i can't stop crying
for no reason at all

cumin
tears
chopped-up jalapeños
tears
canned tomatoes
tears
stirring
tears
stirring
tears
into my frying pan

it feels good
showering in them

soon i will eat them
and they will become
a part of me

suddenly my husband comes
into the apartment

sits me down
and tells me the news

oh
it all makes sense now

i must have felt you
leaving me

each note
a parting
breath

each tear
a step you take away from me

when someone died you'd always
say that the person
"took the train"

patrick iannone

extraordinary musician, cherished husband, loving father, grandfather,
friend to all. a bigger-than-life personality and the ultimate storyteller—
who brought every gathering to life with humor and wit.

which train are you on?
is it making any stops?

if so
i want to get on

pain

become curious about it
get to know it
walk through it

slow

let it pass through you
by you
and back again

junkies and jesus

i was reading bukowski's
love is a dog from hell
on my way to work when

i noticed a card stuffed
inside page 159
it lay over a poem
entitled "junkies"

the poem began

"she shoots up in the neck"

the card
which covered the rest of the poem
read

"a prayer for peace
life is only a dream
we shall awaken
and what a joy!
the greater our sufferings
the more limitless our glory
oh! do not let us waste the trial
jesus sends

as a gift of prayer
in loving memory
patrick iannone"

first i laughed at the
juxtaposition of "junkies"
with this sweet card sent
in honor of my grandfather

then i became envious of those
who believe in god

i ask myself
did fear of death
give birth to religion?

if so
no judgment here

because
i know firsthand

there's only
one thing worse
than death itself
and that is the fear of it

bbbbooooyyyyssss!

she sang
from the top of the staircase

i remember the sound
of feet tearing up the staircase

like bulls running through
the narrow streets of spain
and

crash
the railings
crash
loosening
crash
from the
crash
floor

brothers

brothers are like
animals

i thought
as i lay in bed
staring at the pink-washed walls

winding up the tiny ballerina
that was sitting in my hands

watching it spin
to "waltz of the flowers"

"nnnnoooo!"

i screamed
from across the yard

it was a summer night in july

i watched as they caught the fireflies
snatching them with their hands

putting them between
their thumb and index fingers
and

crush
they
crush
turn into
crush
glitter

painting the ground
with their dead bodies
lighting the cement on fire

brothers are like
animals

i thought
as i made a house out of fallen ivy
for a crew of ants i had befriended

while tiptoeing across the wooden
railroad blocks that kept the
azaleas from overgrowing

i laid honeysuckles down
for them to feed off of
and named them
after the little women

ssssqqqquuuuiiiisssshhhhh!

i was sandwiched between them
in the back of the car

hardly any room to breathe
let alone move a finger

so close
i felt their breath
moving through my body

each inhale
tightening the space between us
and

squish
i become
squish
something of a
squish
human sandwich
squish

ggggaaaasssspppp!

came out of my mouth
we were in the basement
grabbing each other's legs and mowing
the carpet floor like grass

red
raw
knees
he was teaching me
how to maneuver out of
a head lock

squirming like a worm
forcing itself out of the dirt
during a rainfall

squirm
i must
squirm
get out
squirm
before
squirm
my head explodes
squirm

brothers
are like animals

strong
so strong

and hard
hard on the outside

and soft
soft on the inside

disruptive
loud
and
burning up
like wildfire

i wondered what the other girls
did without them

those creatures

wild
but
beautiful

have i outgrown my soul?

what makes me who i am?

i think about who I was
during my teenage years

i felt things then

in my organs
my cells
my insides

powerful
crazy
wild

as i've gotten older
i've become numb

simple
static
detached

what has the world done
to that
tender little girl?

a girl like her, like you, like me

nana spent her whole life in my grandfather's shadow
cooking him only the best things
scrubbing his vegetables clean
pouring marinara sauce with crumbled-up sausage
over his rigatoni and
into a bowl that had been warming in the oven

pop never did any of the things dads do today
so she wiped the baby butts
and taught my mother
how to mend holes in sweaters
and told her that linguine and clams
should be cooked with minced and whole clams

it's been said that she'd sneak in her cigarettes
when pop was on the road with the band
but if anyone asks
you didn't hear it from me

i often wonder what nana could have been
if she'd been born a few decades later
with her handwritten letters in perfect script
and her crisp white shirts
and her beautiful mind

maybe she could've gallivanted
all over new york
waiting in lines at shake shack

maybe she could've been an accountant
she did always take care of the bills
or a poet

oh
they are vast
the could have beens
for a girl like her

part two
you

the daughter of a ceramicist

the daughter of a ceramicist
paints all over the bathroom walls
outlining the flowers on the wallpaper
with pink and blue highlighter

she says it's art
her mother agrees

the daughter of a ceramicist
takes her first sip of wine from a glass
belonging to a musician who fell asleep
on her living room couch

she says the booze helps her make art
her mother agrees

the daughter of a ceramicist
takes self-portraits nude
uncovered and sprawled out on
the cement floor
and shows them to strangers on park avenue south

she says it's art
her mother agrees

the daughter of a ceramicist
kisses boys
and kisses girls
one after the other
regardless of whose heart she might break

she says one must feel loved
to do art
her mother agrees

the daughter of a ceramicist
eats only pears from morning to night
she breaks them in half with her hands
and licks the juice off her arm

she says eating anything else
distracts from the art
her mother agrees

the daughter of a ceramicist
can do almost anything
except for one thing

the daughter of a ceramicist
must never

ever

ever

break one of her mother's pots

they say we're wild girls

with big noses
or plumped-up lips

spaces in between
our middle teeth
or perfectly white

d-size boobs
or completely flat

rolls
or bones

and hearts on sleeves
or hearts closed off

having sex
in the back of cars
at 14 years old

or staying a virgin
waiting for that one perfect guy
to come along

we're drunk
and not remembering
and
crushed-up pills
in pretty lines

we're dancing
dancing
dancing
with hands in the air

or we're sitting with folded legs
tapping our toes
quiet
soft

we're the ones
with red lips
and cigarettes
and fucked-up bangs
and fuck-yous

we're the ones with
pink pussy hats on the
streets of new york

with signs glued to our fingers
even after the protest has ended

or we're the ones hiding in houses
writing all the sad poems
clicking on our computer keys
unnoticed or overlooked

we're
gluten-free
or carb-heavy

eyelash extensions
or bare freckles

delicate hands
or roughed-up ones

we're sweet
or salty

large
or
small

tough
so tough

or soft
so soft

they say we're wild
wild wild wild
like a bengal tiger
uncontrollable
and
rebellious

they say we're wild
wild wild wild
like prey
slow
and
meek

they say we're wild girls
but wild girls should be free

when you learned how to love

during the summers
your parents would send you to
uncle moose's

to the house that
sat by the lake
near the woods
and right smack in
the middle of nowhere

it was there
where you learned how to love

alone
you walked through the woods
and taught yourself
the names of different flowers and trees
fern
oak
and
the pink lady's slipper

it was there
where you picked up tiny frogs
and examined the patterns on their bellies
fiery red and spotted black

it was there
where you saw the beauty of a
fawn trailing behind its mother
quietly

jane goodall was your god
and you'd been watching
television shows about animals
gravity
and how many times the earth
circles the sun

it was there
where you saw an experiment
you decided to try

you'd catch a butterfly
and then pin its wings to a canvas
and hang it up in your room

and so you waited patiently
and caught one
the brightest blue
as delicate as filo dough

and you poked a hole in
the upper left corner of its wing
and you watched it flutter
softly
buzzing
then stop
moving altogether

it was then
in the stillness
where you learned how to love

after all these years
this story
is the only one
you haven't told me
more than once

the story of the butterfly
in the summer of '64

with baby

they say when you're pregnant
you're like an emotional sponge

attuned to everything

not only are you carrying
this other person

but you're carrying
the weight of everyone
around you

you are as close to godly
as you'll ever be

everyone's dad is dying

and i'm thinking about
you and me in the front yard

carving pumpkins and pulling
seeds out

slimy

the cold air
dancing through our arms

the smell
of roasting seeds

your hand over mine
as we pour
more salt than mom would have allowed

everyone's dad is dying

and i'm thinking about you
holding my hand
at 5, at 11, at 29

you are motorcycles
and vintage cameras
and dirt on your hands

you are stopping for
mcdonald's french fries
on the way to violin class

you are pistachio ice cream
and rubbing mom's brittle hands
when they hurt

you are a dog by your side
and a shovel in your hand

you are waiting for me
outside
when i pull into the driveway

and you are "don't leave"
even after i've spent the weekend

everyone's dad is dying

beautiful ones

the one whose coat smells like firewood

and the one who knows which way the wind
is heading in the morning

the one who makes lasagna
on sundays
with calloused hands

and the one whose beard
scratches your cheek
when he kisses you hello
and goodbye

the one whose
jean shirts are worn out
in all the right places

and the one who teaches
you the folk songs

the one who shows you
the right way to punch

and the one whose feet
you stand upon
and dance

everyone's dad is dying

beautiful ones

and all i want to say is

stay right here
where i can see you

the roofer and the palm reader

i meet you on the train
you are dirty
callouses on your knuckles
the day's work under your nails

i tilt my head down
so we don't make eye contact
and i try hard not to touch
the pole
or breathe the same air as you

we're swaying back and forth
with the energy of the train
it's an art, this dance

suddenly we take a sharp turn
i'm ready to tumble

when you reach out to catch me
and tell me to hold on

something my dad would say

you ask what i do for work
"i'm a writer," i say
"i thought so," you reply

i scan my hands for ink marks
run my hands
through my hair
checking for pens

"i'm writing a book," i say
"how many pages?" you ask

you continue to tell me
about a great marketing tactic

all it takes
you say
is having a lot of friends
all you do is
tell your friends
to tell their friends
and you'll be good to go

meanwhile
i'm counting all my friends in my head
and thinking

there's no way this will work

somehow
we get to talking

you're a roofer
which explains your dirty fingernails

your wife
she's a palm reader

"it's all bullshit!"
you say

you would know
a guy came to your house
and you watched the kids in the other room
as he told your wife his marriage was in shambles

she could fix it
all he had to do was take a glass of water
that she'd blessed
and put it under his bed

and would you know it?
it worked!
at least that's what the man believed
because that night he and his wife had good sex
and kissed each other goodbye in the morning

you say
"she didn't do shit!
you see? it's all such bullshit!"

and i say
"the mind does crazy things
all it takes is believing in something"

you say
"the only person who can fix us
is god"

i look at you
and say
"isn't god bullshit too?
he's like your wife's fraternal twin"

"there's got to be someone up there,"
you say

"so you're telling me
your wife just made 5 grand off of
a sad man
who wasn't having enough sex
by spitting in a glass of water
and telling him to put
it under his bed

and you believe in god?"

i'm closing my eyes
it's nighttime
and i keep thinking

the mind does crazy things
all it takes is believing in something

dogs

this isn't loyalty
it's not even love
it's some kind of thing
that doesn't exist in words

the way you wait
silently
for me to come back

my school is in the news

when you're growing up
everyone tells you to

stand tall
speak up
fill a room

go big
be strong
chin up
shoulders back

show 'em
what you've got

but no one teaches you
how to be small

because no one imagines
you'll want to fit inside the
littlest crack
on your classroom's wall

or contort
your body
into the tiniest pretzel

or into crumbs
that don't make any sound
when you step on them

no one imagines
you'll want to become
the littlest ball
and roll
down the hallway

roll, roll, roll
all the way home

that you'll want to shrivel up
like a prune
under your teacher's desk

and hold your breath
so that nothing escapes you
not even a whisper

no one imagines you'll wish for
your chest to stop

rising

and

falling

if only for a few moments
so that you might trick them

kids these days
are playing
the shittiest game
of hide-and-seek

while the rest of the world
sits
watching them
trying
their best
to
d i s a p p e a r

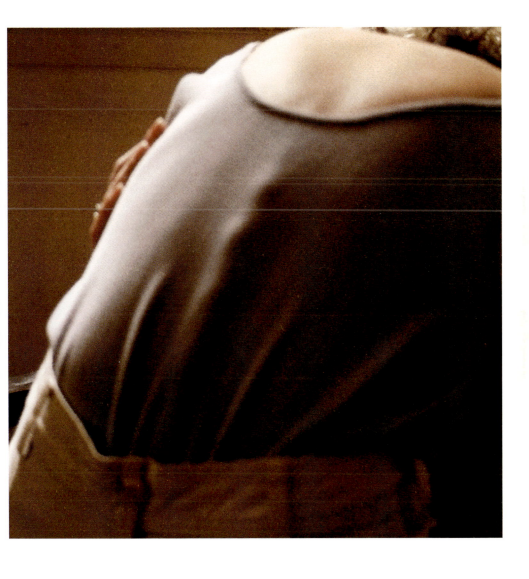

bones and empty stomachs

i don't know you
but we exchanged smiles
and i believe that
counts for something

remember?

the sun was pouring in from the bay
you had a stack of chocolate-chip pancakes
in front of you
a side of bacon
hash browns with old bay seasoning
a large plastic cup of oj

you ordered it because
it was a meal your dad would be proud of

he's next to you
burly
wise looking

let's put it this way
i wouldn't fuck with him

he's got that look
that stance

a big dude
with blue eyes

he's watching you
like a hawk
or maybe like a seagull
if we're trying to set the scene

you hand the little boy next to you
a hundred-dollar bill

he might be
your brother
your nephew
or your son

when the first breeze of the morning
comes to rescue us from the swelter

you say to the little boy
with strawberry-blond hair
and neon shorts

"now, don't you dare
let that money go.
it'll fly away
just like forrest gump's feather"

that's when
our eyes meet

and we share that kind of soft laugh
that only strangers share

then back to my acai bowl i go
and back to googling
the right way to say "acai"

back to taking a
blissful photo of my mother
in front of her short-stack special
blueberry and drowning in syrup

suddenly i hear a sound
coming from your direction
different
hoarse and sickly

loud
so loud

crisp and deep
and from the bottom of your gut

your head in your hands
you're trying to breathe

no one
is looking your way

not the burly man
not the little boy
not the
one
two
three
four
five
people
who surround you at the table

no

it's just you
clutching your chest
struggling
to
breathe

struggling
to keep your
short stacks
down

to keep your
bacon
at bay

to keep your
hash browns
from coming

up
up
up

**i spent my life
tiptoeing around mom**

i never knew
what i was going to get

and i'm not talking
about chocolates

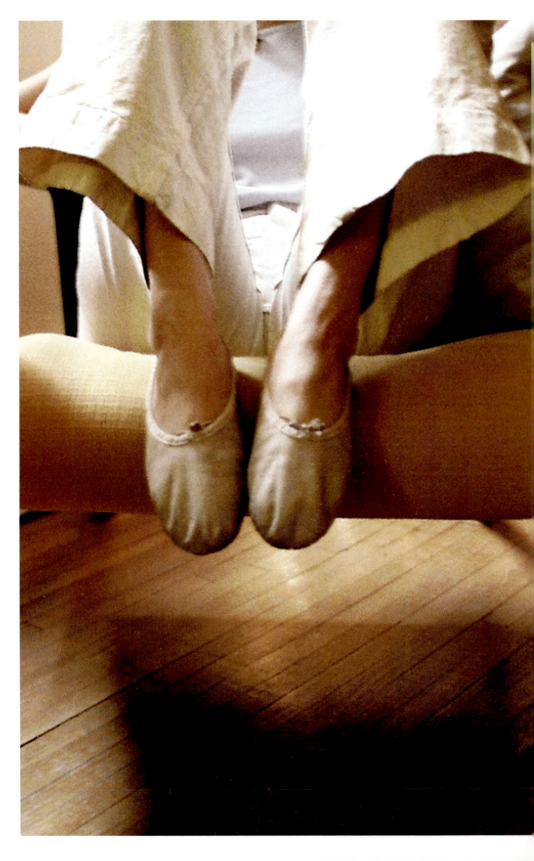

the woman at monmouth racetrack

"i'll show you the secret bathroom
that no one knows about
no lines
no nothing"

i follow you
we zigzag around the racetrack
up and down
through dark tunnels
littered with italian hot dogs
and crumpled-up betting slips

"i just won 150 dollars"
i say
"i put 5 dollars on uncle al"

i only go by the names of horses
not their numbers
that's what i was taught, anyway

this horse was nothing special
but had the same name as pop's brother

the one who would sit in a big recliner
at my grandparents'
so that i could comb his hair
back and forth
and up like einstein

i liked to make it look as crazy as possible
and when i felt good about it
i'd take a picture with my fisher-price camera

he smelled like something familiar
a mix of paul sebastian cologne
and talcum powder
he was gentle with soft eyes
and fuzzy sweaters
i remember
being drawn to him

while we are peeing beside each other
you say you are happy for me
that i've won

you have been coming to the racetrack
every week
for 15 years
and have never won a penny

i say goodbye and
walk back to my seat
past the horses lined up
their heads peeking through metal gates
being pat on the head
by little boys and girls

i suppose for
the woman at monmouth racetrack
having a little hope
is worth more than having
5 dollars in your pocket

sabrina's dream

buddy was in my dream last night
she tells me

he was wearing a yellow sweater
and sitting on a wooden chair in the kitchen
he was really skinny and didn't talk
but then i said hello to him and
he somehow knew who i was
and he
kissed and kissed and kissed
my cheek

it felt really nice

the compassionate doctor

says he doesn't like to give

false hope
or false despair

he waits
for the patient
to ask the questions

and if there's a cup
he chooses half full

tommy the fisherman

you don't keep time
you only keep eyes
on the tide

in and out
low or high
chilly to warm

your eyes
might get cloudy

your skin thin
and burnt
by the sun

your hands
might get worn

like the

bottom of your
boat

the dolphins are known
to massage themselves on

the water that spins out
from your engine

and you wait for them to come
closer

playful

and you smile

you don't keep a watch
because the sea is the time

never-ending
and always

dating in 2018

it's not enough to google his name
and study his profile on
3 different applications

it's not enough to look for
humor
good spelling
pictures of him with dogs
fishing on the delaware river

or if you're lucky
shirtless on the beach

or even better
next to
his mom
or niece

that's always a good sign

or is it?

it's not enough to have long
conversations by text
while you decipher emojis

it's not enough to
squeeze the best parts of yourself
into no more than 5 words
so as to not lose his attention

and it's not enough
to have the perfect first date
your lips kissing his

the nights turned to mornings
the "it hasn't felt this good in a while"

the hoping and the opening
and closing of your heart

it's not enough

you have to be willing to
scan his left ring finger
for an indent

wandering girl

you got bored
watching your brother play soccer
so you wandered into the woods

you spotted
a wolf
eating out of a garbage can

you didn't run
you didn't scream

you paused
took a breath

and howled
arh-wooooooooooooooooooooo
in your little-girl voice

he
howled back
arh-wooooooooooooooooooooo

when you got home
you told your mom
the story

she rolled her eyes
laughed it off
and went back to folding laundry

wandering girl
may you continue to search

for magic
between the pines

acceptance

a son
calls his father
and says

"i'm gay"

his father
says
"what else is new?"

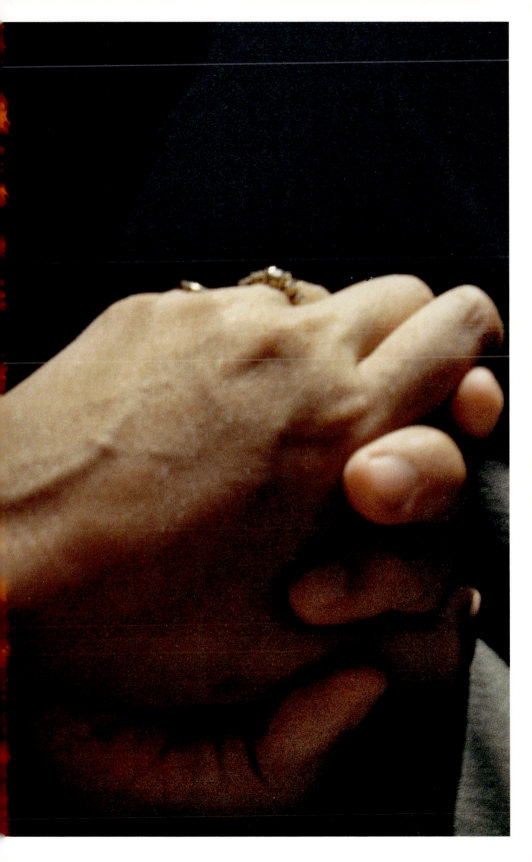

who woke you up this morning?

you wear a brown polo sweater
dusty
and an old school cap
herringbone

the wind you carry
smells of cigarettes
as you pass by

you're a gospel singer
and your buddy
who used to harmonize with you
has passed away from cancer

it was only
a few months back
you and he were
shuffling from train to train

singing
slow
and
loud

now it's just you

alone
and
soft

you've taken in your friend's kids
you feed them
clothe them
and make sure they go to school

you're trying your best

a bright-silver bag
hangs from your arm
metallic and sparkling

and you sing to us

"this little light of mine
i'm gonna let it shine
this little light of mine
i'm gonna let it shine"

your voice
is delicate
withering

it's the saddest sound
in the world

there's nothing
to offer

no cash
no food
no pennies
no nothing

we're listening to drake
on our headphones
and tapping our phones
rapidly
and tucking our noses
into books
and shifting our eyes down

you shuffle along
barely lifting your feet
the song gets muffled
as you walk farther away

"who woke you up this morning?
god woke me up this morning
who woke you up?
god woke me up"

you sing

waiting for someone to listen
waiting for someone to listen

eduard the artist

we don't speak
the same language

you're an oil painter
from russia

and i'm a poet
from new jersey

you're about 90
and i haven't yet turned 30

but that doesn't stop
you from making a drawing
of my sad face

dark-blue veins under my eyes
a tilted beret

i'm looking down at you
while you put pen to paper

words couldn't do this justice

i see in you
what i saw in my grandfather

soft
fragile
talented
gutsy
warm
sensitive

some kind of unimaginable soul

no
we don't speak
the same language

not one lick of the same language

but that doesn't stop us from holding hands
on the first night we meet

i walk you home
through the cold streets of
jersey city

midway
you stop
and offer me
your leather gloves

words couldn't do this justice

when we arrive at your studio
we stay there for four hours

exchanging stories
mostly with our hands

you
point to your heart
and say

tick

tock

tick

tock

and
you point at me

it doesn't take much time
to know what you're saying

sometimes words
aren't enough

sometimes words
aren't necessary

sometimes the faint
clicking of our hearts
is enough

a man and his books

every monday
you sell your books
on the corner of 19th and 7th

lunch poems by frank o' hara
life with picasso
sapiens: a brief history of humankind
mrs. dalloway (i never was a virginia woolf kind of girl)
sometimes sylvia plath

you have good taste

you also have

a gray beard that's yellowed
from your days on the streets

your nose in an edition
of *lolita*

you've probably read it so many times
you've lost count

i wonder
if you're a writer

homeless
and looking for
money

or

maybe as a boy you curled up next to your mom
on nights when you couldn't sleep

she'd read to you
the same story

not once
but three times

four if you were lucky

the more times she'd agree to read to you
the more time you'd have with her next to you

warm

the more time the monsters
would spend in your neighbor's house
instead of making their way over

safe

or maybe you just want to
escape from the world

a world that hasn't
been very good to you

either way it's you who has the story

not those books
not ginsberg
not the people who tiptoe around you
not me
not me writing about you

it's you
who has the story
worth telling

the power of story

"what's your story?"
is a good pickup line

a little interesting
a little mischievous

plus
you'll leave him speechless

what's more exciting than
seeing a man squirm?

peanuts

it takes you a whole 45 minutes
to eat a tiny bag of peanuts

you pick each one up delicately
cherishing it
like how beth in *little women*
cherished butter

we should take lessons from you
the "we" being me
who eats a pound of spaghetti
scooping it into my mouth
with a little ricotta in every bite

or the "we" being he
the guy with the supersized
coke and the #2
because one burger is not enough

or "we" with
the fur coats
and the 40 pairs of shoes
and the gym in our apartment building
the seamless orders
and the cashmere at christmas

all peanuts
compared with
peanuts

the honey-roasted ones
that you've spent your last
two dollars on

cat lady

we pull up to your house
and suddenly
10 pairs of eyes
glowing
appear in the windows
over your porch

we shake hands
i notice your shirt
has a pattern
made of whiskers

and then
i feel
my legs start to itch
and my hands

fleas?

itch
itch
itch

what is it about cats?

itch
itch
itch

and what is it about
writers loving cats?

bukowski
burroughs
twain
hemingway
yeats
dickens
plath

maybe they remind us of ourselves

fucking wild
fucking tired

totally mad
and totally misunderstood

i look into your eyes
as you hand over 5 kittens

and just like that
i've added 5 years to my life
(if what bukowski said is true)

"the more cats you have, the longer you live"

and you
you'll live forever
from the looks of the fleabites
that are creeping up your wrists

hippie girl, mom

hippie girl
mom
the girl with
the flowers in her hair
the tiny soft lips
and the perfectly curved eyebrows
soft
soft

your mom
wanted you to be a secretary

you'd go to typing school
and you'd get married to the nice
italian boy from down the street

and you'd have babies named
pasquale
sofia
angelo
and you'd make them
pastina with chicken broth
and spoon it into their mouths
when they were sick

you'd get married in a big church
with a big band
and you'd stay in that small town
forever

you'd borrow sugar
from your aunt next door
and you'd roll out the dough
for the cookies
and you'd stay
stay

except you didn't

you hitchhiked to colorado
and lived in teepees

you made shirts out of bandanas
snuck into college psychology classes

and wrote letters home
adorned with doodles
of the sun setting over the mountains

you had your first baby
all alone in the hospital
your young body
strong
strong

you strapped him on your back
and went to new york city

and you married the boy
who rode the motorcycle

falling in love while a police song
played in the background

you made ashtrays out of paper
and you
burnt it down
you burnt it all down

all the ideas
all of the ideas
they had for you

hippie girl
mom
the girl with
the flowers in her hair
the tiny soft lips
and perfectly curved eyebrows
soft
soft

one look at you
inspires a poem

i watch you dancing
from across the room

and i see me
in you

me in you

you wild beatnik
you shooting star
you unpredictable storm

you steady tree
rooted firmly in the ground

i look at you
and i see me
in you

me in you

a boy from maine

is building his own house
in carhartt suspenders

a boy from maine
has a motorola flip phone

and uses his ipod
to browse tinder

a boy from maine sexts
a girl from new york

and talks about putting
pickled radishes
on her nipples
and lining her body
with organic carrots

picking them off
one by one

a boy from maine
takes his first shower in 10 days
and moisturizes his face with olive oil

a boy from maine
is not a boy from new york

and no one can tell if that's a good thing
or not

addiction

there's something sadder
than the holes in your arms from needles

it's your eyes

lost

the pizza waitress

it might as well be your home
this tavern
the kind of place
where you park by the window
so you can check up on your car
every once in a while

you've been here for 25 years or
for as long as i can remember

your name is
sheila
donna
or trish

it's rude to ask at this point

you've got long red fiery nails
always done perfectly

and a smock
dusty with remnants of pizza dough

splattered spots
from the little cups of pepperoni
that gather oil

when you walk they change shape
and spill a little bit

you've got a raspy voice
from years of smoking marlboro lights

you've got 3 kids at home
over 30

you say you like it like that

and you've worked every day for
as long as you remember

you say you like it like that

you never ask anything without
saying "sweetie" at some point in the sentence

you say to me, "i'll live till i'm 100,
you know? because i'm tough. i'm tough and i
will never stop working. take my advice, sweetie.
it's good to work. it keeps you strong."

is it weird that i like the smell of your breath?
a subtle blend of coffee and vanilla

you're familiar
and you work harder
than anyone i've ever known

and you serve me all my favorite things

onion blossoms
pepper, potatoes, and eggs
lots of it

but my favorite thing
is our little conversation
between the appetizers
and the pizza

men i trust

1
2
3
4
4.5

farmer mike

lost seven goats to
a pack of black vultures

our feet cold by the
snow beneath us

our breath making
patterns in the air

i ask, "do goats mourn?"

he says
the mother goat spent
a whole year
looking for her two babies
that were eaten alive

their carcasses were dropped
from the sky
but she kept looking

it's true
i suppose

grieving mothers
whether hollow-horned
or made of human
flesh and bone

can
wander
and
watch
and
wait

but they'll never
ever
fill that hole
that absence
that makes a home
in their hearts

time

we're young
and then we're old

we're blond
and then we're gray

we're smooth
and then we're wrinkled

we unwrap the gifts
and then we place them under the tree

we're stacking blocks
and then we're stacking porcelain dishes

we're running marathons
and then we're under hospital sheets

we're reciting pablo neruda
and then we're being told what our names are

we don't know how to speak
and then we can't find the words

we have someone tie our shoes
and then we have someone tie our shoes

we're fed by our mothers
and then we're fed by our children

we have first kisses
and then we have last kisses

and then we're nothing at all

nail polish

you look like a regular old man
balding
a long white beard
a cane balanced between your knees

you rest your chin
gently atop it

that's when i see
your fingernails
painted black and orange

you must have
something important to say

rocky the pennsylvania driver

wears a gold chain
and plays asap rocky
the bass turned up so high
we can hardly hear each other

he says when you have kids
you should be prepared to give up
98% of yourself

the other 2% is for your
sports car
and driving fast

thanks

nick ceglia
mom & dad
casey, jess, dustin & alicia
polina dyer
jake williams
ali burgis
sarah kasbeer
alana salguero
alyssa benjamin
jen zegarra
melissa zahorsky
holly stayton
patience randle
polina dyer of studio p+p

and everyone else who has touched me on this journey.
whose photos are included in this book.
for your stories.
for everything.

about the author

Emmy Marucci was born in West Orange, New Jersey, to a family of artists and storytellers. As a young adult, she moved to New York City, where she began taking nostalgic photos with her 35-millimeter camera and writing for small poetry zines.

Eventually, she helped create *SHK* (*Seen Heard Known*)—a digital fashion magazine—and began writing copy for emerging and established fashion brands, most recently EILEEN FISHER. Emmy's poetry and photography center on the rich sensuousness of childhood and the stories we learn to tell about ourselves and others.

Emmy lives in Jersey City, New Jersey, with her husband, who is also a writer; her three cats, who look exactly alike; shelves of half-alive succulents; and a closet full of her grandfather's shirts.

index

Andrews McMeel Publishing
a division of Andrews McMeel Universal
1130 Walnut Street, Kansas City, Missouri 64106

www.andrewsmcmeel.com

19 20 21 22 23 TEN 10 9 8 7 6 5 4 3 2 1

ISBN: 978-1-4494-9689-0

Library of Congress Control Number: 2019934271

Editor: Melissa R. Zahorsky
Art Director: Diane Marsh
Production Editor: Elizabeth A. Garcia
Production Manager: Carol Coe

Author photo on page 219: Ali Burgis

ATTENTION: SCHOOLS AND BUSINESSES
Andrews McMeel books are available at quantity discounts with bulk purchase for educational, business, or sales promotional use. For information, please e-mail the Andrews McMeel Publishing Special Sales Department: specialsales@amuniversal.com.